STEAM MEMORIES: 1950

No. 16: Nottinghamshire, Derbyshire & Linc

Including: *Nottingham Victoria, Annesley, Grantham, Retford & Lincoln Motive Power Depots*

Book Law Publications

Introduction

Once upon a time, in a belt of prime East Midlands countryside, roughly 40 miles east to west and 35 miles from north to south, and encompassing parts of the counties of Derbyshire, Lincolnshire and Nottinghamshire, we had some of the greatest concentrations of railway lines in the country. The western side of our belt, especially, was thick with dozens and dozens of what would appear to be branch lines. This, of course, was Coal Country - the Nottinghamshire, Derbyshire coalfield - a vast source of wealth for a few but a means of existence and employment for many. A number of the pre-Grouping railways wanted to get into the coalfield and although the Midland entered by some of the prime routes, and enjoyed a couple of decades being the only railway to serve the growing number of pits, others followed by the more difficult and usually expensive means. The Great Northern entered the coalfield properly in the 1870s and twenty years later the Manchester, Sheffield & Lincolnshire consolidated its foothold in the north by building a new main line right through the centre and tapping traffic from existing and newly sunk collieries. To the east of our geographical belt of land, on the extreme edge of the coalfield in question, lies the East Coast Main Line which for much of its length does run through nothing but prime farmland and rural beauty. However, a couple of junctions stand out along the length of line under review - Grantham and Retford. Both of these places feature in our aptly titled album if only to show off some more of the Pacifics which plied that glorious route.

Not strictly inside the geographical boundaries of our imaginary belt but certainly within the county boundaries of Lincolnshire, we pay a short visit to the seaside and then, the extreme south-west of the county at Stamford. The pictures illustrating Derbyshire do not include any which show off the Peak District or indeed anything of what might be termed as the more acceptable face of Derbyshire. Instead we concentrate on the railway infrastructure and the trains.

Hopefully, the section around Nottingham will not appear to be 'just a little too much' as the city did have a comprehensive and historically interesting railway system which still serves the city's inhabitants along with a superb tram system which can only expand to meet the requirements of future, more aware generations.

Most of what is included within these pages is pure, simple history. Not just the locomotives either - lines, routes, stations, commodities, traffic and industry. Enjoy!

(Title page) **Retford - 15th March 1959. Locally allocated Thompson B1 No.61231 restarts a northbound passenger train away from the Down loop and rejoins the Down main at the east-west flat crossing. The vantage point is the landing of the signal box (see following illustration) from where we get a good view of the point rodding and signal wires protecting this vital junction.** *BLP - KRP212.6.*

Printed and bound by The Amadeus Press, Cleckheaton, BD19 4TQ.
First published in the United Kingdom by Book Law Publications, 382 Carlton Hill Nottingham, NG4 1JA.

Retford - February 1959. Looking west along the former Great Central Sheffield-Lincoln main line, we see Robinson J11 No.64315 about to cross the ECML with an Immingham bound freight. Retford South signal box dominates the scene - if ever a signal box was required anywhere, it was at this location. On the extreme left of this view can be seen a rather unusual telegraph pole with quadruple direction arms serving the wires running not only east-west but also north-south - it must have been a linesman's nightmare to maintain. Just below that particular post three 'stored' engines are tucked away on a siding which was connected to the GC line at a point where the brake van of this train is passing. Because space at the depot was at a premium, the siding was a favourite location for Thrumpton engine shed to store locomotives awaiting works or those simply 'laid-up' for lack of work. On this particular day two Gresley O2s and J11 were the occupants. The gradient posts on the ECML read: 1 in 1348 descending southwards and 1 in 1635 ascending northbound. That appertaining to the east-west line reads 1 in 146 ascending westwards and dead level eastbound. The ground disc signal facing the Down traffic on the ECML is positioned alongside the Up main whilst a twin signal, on the west side of the Down line, points in the Up direction (see previous illustration). Both these signals apparently enabled 'wrong-line running' on the ECML whenever a 'side' of the flat crossing was taken out for maintenance or other situations. Note that the disc signal had no counterparts on the east-west route. On the right can be seen a group of 'spotters' congregated on the subway parapet wall. The subway was the only way for pedestrian traffic to traverse the ECML in the vicinity of the station and it was frequently used by enthusiasts making their way to the former Great Northern engine shed which is hidden behind the signal box. The British Locomotive Shed Directory states the walking route from the station to the GN shed as: *Turn right outside the station, and almost immediately turn right again into a subway running under the railway...... Walking time 5 minutes.* BLP - KRP 207.6.

Off to do some work at a 'local' colliery, J6 No.64178 has just departed from Thrumpton shed, collected a brake van and is now approaching the ECML flat crossing before proceeding west towards Worksop in February 199. *BLP - KRP 208.2.*

4

Retford - February 1959. Bathed by the midday sun, a respectable looking Thompson B1 No.61208 simmers outside the engine shed at Thrumpton in February 1959. The usual fare offered at this depot was freight locomotives of both 0-6-0 and 2-8-0 types with the latter, made up of Gresley O2s and variants of Robinson O4s, dominating the allocation. Although some distance apart (fifteen minutes brisk walk), and run independently of each other duty wise, the two engine sheds at Retford shared the same code - 36E - during BR days. They also had the same Shed Master in charge of both establishments. From its entry into traffic in July 1947, this B1 spent the next eighteen years working from Retford shed(s) until forced to transfer to Doncaster when Retford depot closed in June 1965. *BLP - KRP 207.5.*

The former Great Northern Railway engine shed at Retford during the final decade of steam on BR. A couple of Thompson B1s, No.61231 and an unidentified member hiding from the daylight, share the place with a Haymarket based Gresley A3, No.60094 COLORADO, which appears to be, perhaps, not as well as it could be. The date of the picture is somewhat obscure but is thought to be about December 1958, shortly after the A3 had been fitted with ATC/AWS equipment at Doncaster works. No.60094 would have run down to Barkston triangle most probably during the testing of the new safety equipment and may have called into Retford with a minor problem. There is no record of anything untoward taking place so, whatever caused the Pacific to visit 36E might remain lost in the mists of time. *BLP - KRP246.8.*

Deltic approaches Retford from the south on a wild but sunny February day in 1958. The big diesel is still showing its paces to British Railways and this lightweight load of just seven coaches should not be anything but easy for the 'World's most powerful single unit diesel locomotive' as the Co-Co was marketed by its makers English Electric. Of course the 3,300 horsepower contained within the stylised body of the locomotive was the most powerful at the time and its twin Napier Deltic diesel engines were unique in railway application. *BLP - KRP208.*

Back at the station, on the last day of March 1958, the pace of traffic was warming up and local resident J6 No.64174 waits for a clear road behind the southbound express which is thundering through on the Up fast, hauled by A3 No.60041 SALMON TROUT. Note the vertical white stripes on the door and end of the ventilated van behind the J6 - was this a shock absorbing van with extra tall striping ? The design of the vehicle appears to be pre-British Railways but who knows - this writer would be obliged if a reader could enlighten him further. *BLP - KRP213.1.*

Having stopped at Retford to pick up some intending passengers, A3 No.60103 FLYING SCOTSMAN sets out from the Up platform with an afternoon express bound for King's Cross on Saturday, 10th May 1958. Having transferred from Grantham shed just over a year previously, the A3 had settled in at King's Cross shed and it was to stay there until withdrawn for preservation nearly five years after this scene was captured on film. Once this train had set off there was a lull until the next express thundered through. Most of the freight traffic had ceased by lunchtime and only those light engines making their way home to the former GC shed ventured over the flat crossing in a west-east direction. Any shunting which might have taken place at the station or the adjacent yards has ceased for the weekend. Nevertheless, the warmth of the afternoon, the smell of that smoke and the elegance of the Pacific put you into a comfort zone for a few tranquil moments before the signal box bells started off again to warn of another imminent main line arrival. *BLP - KRP221.3.*

Whisker Hill, Retford - Friday, 4th April 1958. Staveley based O4/7 No.63772 waits patiently by the signal box at Whisker Hill junction ahead of a Down freight train as Thompson B1 No.61231 comes off the loop line after a Retford station stop with a westbound excursion (No.970). Just before that event, a Sheffield-Lincoln stopping train, headed by B1 No.61258, diverged onto the loop for its Retford stop. Most of the traffic on the loop consisted passenger trains, much of the goods traffic passing through Retford took either west to east, east to west, north to south or south to north paths, only a minority changing direction from say west to south or vice versa. We have seen the B1 in an earlier view featuring Retford's former GN engine shed but the 2-8-0 is a new sighting. These two locomotives had a couple of things in common; both were built by North British Locomotive Co. in Glasgow, albeit some thirty-five years apart, and both were cut up at Doncaster 'Plant' works. Ironically, the oldest engine outlasted the younger B1 by about eight months. Other than those two facts the pair never crossed paths other than in traffic as here. They never visited the same works for overhauls and were never allocated to the same depots. No.63772 spent its first thirty years of life as a 'bog standard' O4 (8K) then, after rebuilding it worked for another twenty-one years before being condemned. *BLP - KRP214.2.*

Something of a study in light and shade this one. The mood of winter is being replaced by the softer light of springtime as A4 No.60026 MILES BEEVOR races south over the Idle bridge with a Newcastle-King's Cross express on 15th March 1959. Still swollen from weeks of rains and snow melt, the smooth waters of the river give us a perfect reflection of the bridge and the background foliage. Having no brick parapets, and relying on railings for safety, the open aspect of the bridge allows us to observe the wheels and motion of the locomotive as it is frozen in the split second of time, caught on film by the camera. This river bank was a favourite spot for Keith Pirt and over the years of his visits he managed to capture every seasonal change and the moods that accompanied them. There was an element of peace to be had at this place - in between trains. Many photographers sought out their own favourite spot from where to capture the passing trains and this particular place was claimed by KRP on many of his visits to Retford. Later during the afternoon of the 15th March, the sun broke through the cloud base and out came Keith's colour camera to record some memorable views across the water meadows. *BLP - KRP212.7.*

Shortly after the A4 had disappeared into the mist on that fifteenth day of March 1959, a filthy and unidentified V2 came rushing up from the south with a heavy express. Where the train was headed is not logged but the carriages were carrying nameboards, which did not mean a lot as this was the ECML and many of the express trains carried them so identifying a particular express can be difficult. *BLP - KRP212.8.*

It is easy to forget how much freight was moved by British Railways. Even in April 1958, ten years after the formation of BR and the post-war explosion of private road haulage, our railway system bore the blunt of the goods movement throughout the UK. However, that was changing daily in favour of the road lorries. As each 'anti-railway' government came into power they cut the budget of the organisation and in doing so prevented investment in some of the more critical areas. It might be argued that BR built dozens of new mechanised marshalling yards, and that, along with new rolling stock and a plethora of new standard locomotives would surely ensure a victory for BR over the road hauliers. However the road boys were not burdened with the rules, regulations and Acts of Parliament that BR had to contend with before they could hope to compete. We watched the slow death of BR's goods services as each was either snatched away by the 'enemy' or thrown away by successive boards and civil servants who either had no interest in the survival of the railways or were under the orders of their masters to 'get rid as soon as possible'. This illustration shows how BR used to move, with apparent ease, long steel sections in 1958: Lowmac wagon as a barrier for overhanging load, bogie bolster with load, Lowmac or similar for overhang, ditto, loaded bogie bolster, Lowmac; ditto, etc. Easy. The length of the train is unknown but it could be any number of vehicles. No one is inconvenienced. We have one crew. I know we have been here before but put this lot on the road and problems arise immediately. Common sense is once again trodden down by wanton greed or sheer madness. Handling this southbound train past Ordsall with apparent ease is J39 No.64898. *BLP - KRP214.6.*

13

Friday, 23rd May 1959, Grantham station, north end, late afternoon. A4 No.60020 GUILLEMOT, one of Gateshead's finest - okay so they were all dirty - runs into the Up platform with a King's Cross bound express. Its quite probable that the A4 will come off here and its place taken by another - probably cleaner - Pacific but just look at that head of steam. The schoolboys have probably been home already, grabbed a bite, along with their note books, and run down to the station to catch the evening trade on the ECML. At least some of them appear happy to see the grubby A4, no doubt the fireman is happy to see Grantham too. Because of its Tyneside allocation, this A4 was coupled to the same non-corridor tender (No.5669) throughout its life as it would not be required to work the non-stops between London and Edinburgh. However, it did work such prestige BR trains as the TALISMAN which changed engines at Newcastle. Pre-war it also took its turn on the likes of the SILVER JUBILEE albeit smartly turned out for the occasions. *BLP - KRP224.6*

Another Tyneside engine at Grantham on that Friday evening in May 1959 was Heaton A3 No.60085 MANNA which had followed GUILLEMOT in with another express from the north. Here amongst the debris littering the shed yard, the engine has been coaled, watered and turned - just the fire and ashpan to clean now before No.60085 is ready to work back home. This was yet another Gresley Pacific which had spent its whole life working from Tyneside depots, either Gateshead or Heaton. It had been at the latter shed since August 1944 and its external appearance gives a clue to that fact. Grantham was a superb place to observe railway operations and trainspot too. Many 'expresses' changed engines here so that you usually got two Pacifics for the price of one. Of course there were those expresses that did not stop at Grantham and watching those trains hammer through the place was 'icing on the cake' so to speak. *BLP - KRP 225.3.*

This panoramic view of the southern end of Grantham, on a lovely warm evening in June 1959, captures A4 No.60007 at the head of an Up express shortly after departing for King's Cross. An interesting observation in the October 1954 Railway Observer stated that Grantham, with a population of only 23,000, enjoyed the service of no fewer than twelve express trains from London every weekday, making not more than one intermediate stop, during the current winter timetable. By comparison Birmingham (pop. 1,112,000) was served by just eight such trains; Bristol (442,000) had four; Nottingham (306,000) three; Leicester (285,000) eight; Coventry (258,000) four; Derby (141,000) two; Norwich (121,000) three; Peterborough (45,000) ten; Rugby (45,000) fourteen. Lincoln, it was pointed out, had no express service for its 69,000 population but had a through service which took 3 hours 12 minutes including a dreary twenty-one minute wait at - Grantham. *BLP - KRP230.6.*

The A4 - and still the fastest steam locomotive in the world - No.60022 MALLARD takes a leisurely run around the turning triangle at Grantham engine shed in March 1960. Obviously ex-works, the Pacific may well have been on a running-in turn from Doncaster before being released into traffic. The date coincides with No.60022 having just finished a General overhaul at the Plant in readiness for the seasonal build up in passenger traffic on the ECML. At the same overhaul a speed indicator was fitted on the left side of the engine. Grantham's coaling plant appears to have given MALLARD some choice lumps of coal which was only to be expected as this particular depot serviced and turned some of the Eastern Region's premier express passenger locomotives. The turning triangle at Grantham was installed during 1951 when the depot's 70ft turntable, or rather the foundation of which, was becoming problematic again after temporary measures had been take to remedy subsidence from about 1947 onwards. The triangle, situated west of the depot, was not a simple triangular formation of track - room for such a luxury was not available at Grantham - so a novel, and perhaps unique, solution was to install a scissors crossover at the south end of the land so that in plan form the turning facility looked like an open pair of scissors joined at the handles. In this view No.60022 was actually moving forwards towards the western extremity of the triangle prior to reversing along the 'join' which connected with the eastern extremity of the triangle. Once it was at the latter spot it could move forwards along the scissors arm to the point of the installation. The business end of the engine was then heading north. Besides being an essential and necessary part of the depot's facilities, Grantham's triangle was a useful place to take photographs of solo locomotives without the usual 'clutter' found on shed yards. *BLP - KRP290.7.*

The former Great Northern engine shed at Lincoln became the 'head shed' of the 40 group of motive power depots in 1948. It had under its authority as 40A such places as Immingham and Langwith Junction and, from 1958, the likes of Colwick. British Railways spent a lot of money rebuilding the actual shed, basically starting where the LNER had finished their remodelling of the depot layout and facilities. In this late May 1960 view, resident B1 No.61006 BLACKBUCK, looking fresh and clean after a General overhaul at Doncaster, and Immingham based O4 No.63707 (in the right background) are stabled on the sidings put down by the LNER in the 1930s on reclaimed land at the south side of the shed. For its size, Lincoln was well blessed with engine sheds - four in fact at Grouping - the city's geographical position being the meeting place of the Great Central, Great Eastern, Great Northern and Midland railways. The first to go after Grouping was the former GER establishment at Pyewipe, the LNER rightly believing that two sheds could sustain its motive power requirements in the city. The LMS kept the small shed St Marks going to service their goods and passenger services emanating from Nottingham and west thereof. During the depressed period of the Thirties' the LNER, with Government help, invested large sums in the Holmes depot and a mechanical coaling plant, and a revised layout with ashpits and a new 65ft turntable. The area formerly occupied by the old coaling stage, adjacent to the engine shed, was cleared and a building to house a wheel drop was built. As the LNER modernisation came to its conclusion at the Holmes, the exGCR engine shed closed in May 1939 although the by now roofless shed building there was used to stable locomotives throughout the war period and afterwards until it became a carriage shed and later a diesel multiple unit depot. St Marks shed went in 1959 when BR realised the duplication of stabling sheds was excessive even by their corporate standards. What of the unkempt forty-five years old 2-8-0? Well, in September 1960 it was sent to Gorton where it was given a Heavy Intermediate overhaul which then kept it in traffic until mid-1965, when it was working from Colwick. The much younger 4-6-0 was condemned in September 1963, not quite twenty years old! *BLP - DHB3284.*

Crossing the bridge over the Upper Witham river at Lincoln in July 1960, B1 No.61258 makes its way to Central station to work a westbound service. East Holmes Junction signal box stands to the extreme left and beyond that is the engine shed where this 4-6-0 had been a resident since June 1952. As can be gleaned from the external condition of engine and tender, the pair had recently enjoyed a General overhaul at Doncaster 'Plant' works so mechanically the B1 should also be in fine fettle. Note the tender, No.4095 of the coal weighing type and coupled to No.61258 since a 'General' at Doncaster on October 1955. One of only four scattered about the B1 class, this particular tender remained coupled to the 4-6-0 until both were cut up at Doncaster in March 1964 wherein another distinction brings No.61258 to the fore: it was the last B1 to be cut up at Doncaster works. However, getting back to the illustration, we assume that the B1 was probably off to take out a passenger working to Sheffield, perhaps the Harwich-Liverpool boat train because the usual 'Brit' was ailing. Who knows. What is just about factual is the coal or rather coal dust and slack piled on the tender - the fireman has got his work cut out with that lot. *BLP - DHB3987.*

19

Look no hands! J39 No.64726 turns on the Lincoln table with apparent ease as the crew sit in the cab during a warm day in July 1960. Obviously coaled and watered, the locally based 0-6-0 is ready for its next turn of duty. The engine did not however have much longer to go before it was called into Doncaster for a heavy overhaul but was instead condemned when it got to the Plant works. No.64726 was one of the 159 J39s which received General overhauls at Derby works under the British Railways Inter Regional Assistance scheme of 1951. Its last 'General' was done at Stratford in 1956 so its boiler was ready for changing. The 'no hands' trick was being performed by the vacuum tractor hidden behind the tender and being tended to by the fireman with no effort at all. Situated between the engine shed and the coaling plant, the 65ft diameter turntable was one of the enhancements installed at Lincoln shed in 1938, along with a mechanical coaling plant and a wheel drop, the latter on the site of the old turntable at the north-east corner of the engine shed. *BLP - DHB3984.*

Thompson rules! At least in this picture taken at Lincoln engine shed in July 1960. Two of Edward Thompson's more acceptable, and agreeable looking products - his O1 class 2-8-0 and the ubiquitous B1 4-6-0. The former of course, represented here by No.63646, was a rebuild of numerous Robinson O4s undertaken during WW2 and afterwards at Gorton works. Standardisation was Thompson's aim with LNER locomotive policy and he certainly managed that with the 4-6-0s. Of those classes introduced by earlier Chief Mechanical Engineers, he rebuilt a number of them too in order to standardise as much as possible. The B17 Part 6, the two cylinder rebuild of the B17 class, the B2, and the B16 Part 3, are three types which got his attention. However, it was the B1 which was the real gem in his crown. Over four hundred were built during an eight year period which encroached into the BR era by two and half years, virtually to the eve of BR locomotive standardisation. At the core of all these engines was the Diagram 100A boiler which was, besides those classes already mentioned, fitted to B3 Part 3, O2 Part 4 and O4 Part 8. *BLP - DHB3982.* 21

A close up of the swing bridge at Holmes East Junction which carried the main line over the Upper Witham and past the engine shed at Lincoln. This time, also in July 1960, a rather grotty J11, No.64284, is traversing the appliance. Note the water level of the river, even in summer. The railways here have been prone to flooding since their arrival in the city but luckily over the decades very little damage has resulted from numerous inundations. Note the corner of the well lit wheel-drop building on the left of the picture. *BLP - DHB3986.*

The railway facilities at Sutton-on-Sea were created by the grandly titled Sutton & Willougby Railway & Dock Company which was incorporated in July 1884 to build a line from Sutton to Willoughby and which opened at the end of September 1886. Less than two years later a connection was completed northwards to the existing terminus at Mablethorpe and a 22½ mile loop line, with six intermediate stations, connecting Louth with Willoughby via the coast was created. From the outset the Great Northern Railway provided the motive power for the line but did not fully absorb the whole route until March 1902. Being both the earlier station and the largest in terms of facilities, complete with engine shed (actually closed in 1924) and turntable, Mablethorpe (population 2,832 in 1927) gave its name to the Loop. Sutton-on-Sea, although enjoying excellent beaches did not quite reach the 'grandiose' heights of its larger neighbour. Nevertheless, the place was well served by local and through passenger services such as this Grimsby-Peterborough via Boston train in 1961. Most of the local services had actually given over to diesel multiple units when Louth engine shed closed in December 1956 and this particular train was one of the few which was still regularly steam hauled at the time. Boston based Ivatt mogul No.43147 has charge of this late afternoon service which, in locomotive terms, was 'a bit of a dawdle' and not one to catch if you wanted to get anywhere fast. The Cl.4 2-6-0 was an orphan from the Midland & Great Northern closure (note the tablet exchanging apparatus recessed into the tender, next to the cab) and had arrived at Boston shed from Melton Constable in February 1959 to join twenty-odd other members of the class allocated to the place. On reaching Boston, this train would have an engine change, using a New England locomotive. This Boston engine, which had worked up to Grimsby with an early morning goods train, would retire to the shed. Note the GN somersault signal (No.14) pegged for the off. Also of note is the station name totem fixed to the concrete fence post at waist level. The goods yard was served by a daily (except weekends) pick-up from Boston, the Saturday service during the summer was suspended to allow the various excursions a clear path as they brought day trippers and holiday makers to the resort or Mablethorpe. The station closed in October 1970 along with the remaining stations on the Loop. *BLP - DDLMS125.* 23

In June 1958 the C12 'Atlantic' tanks which had worked the Stamford-Essendine service since 1920 were running on borrowed time. This is No.67394 en route from Stamford (Town) with a passenger working to Essendine. The original terminus of the Essendine trains was Stamford (East) but that station's closure in March 1957 saw the former GN services diverted to the one-time Midland Railway station known as Town. The train is running over MR metals at this point, with the C12 running onto the connection and about to join the course of the LNER Stamford (East) to Essendine line. Stamford East signal box stands on the right, guarding the junction where the tracks from East station join from the right. Initially the Great Northern Railway allocated three of these 4-4-2Ts to Stamford engine shed [which stood behind the photographer on the north side of the line], and they worked the services to Wansford and Essendine but when the former route was abandoned in July 1929, just a pair of the elegant Ivatt designed tank engines were required. When the exLNER East station closed, the engine shed also lost its status and became merely a stabling point although in the years leading up to closure, the engines were all supplied by New England shed on a fortnightly rotation of duties. Apparently the last C12 to work the Stamford-Essendine service was No.67398 which returned to New England from its Stamford stint in October 1958. Its replacement (the S&E trains still had another ten months to run) was ex Great Central N5 No.69293 which had transferred to the Peterborough depot on 27th April last, from Chester. So, perhaps unfittingly, the last locomotives to work the Essendine services from Stamford were not those from the original parent company but instead it was a sixty-three years old Manchester, Sheffield & Lincolnshire Railway 0-6-2T which had spent most of its long life working the Cheshire Lines. *BLP - DHB 753.*

Stamford, Lincolnshire, 27th September 1965. With less than a week to go before the abolition of the Seaton-Stamford push-pull service, an early afternoon train waits at Stamford for its next run westward to Seaton, propelled by an Ivatt 2-6-2T. Leicester provided the motive power for these p&p services but in actuality Market Harborough shed took care of the engines needs, including overnight stabling and weekend washouts. Until October 1960 the branch engines lodged during the week at the tiny wooden shed at Seaton but when that establishment closed (the only engine shed located within the county of Rutland which is not within the remit of the title of this album so we'll hear no more about it!), with the ending of the passenger service over the branch between Seaton and Uppingham, the engine ran to Market Harborough each night. Besides working the scant passenger service, the branch engine also worked a daily goods up to Uppingham until that service too was withdrawn in June 1964. At the time it was withdrawn, this particular push & pull service was the last of its kind running on British Railways: Ivatt 2-6-2T No.41212 apparently worked the last trains. The fireman leans into the window of the driving compartment, no doubt reflecting with the driver on the coming cessation of the Stamford service and the future prospects for advancement of footplate staff in the area. Redundancy was probably the only option open. *BLP - DDLMS153.*

25

The motive power for the Stamford-Seaton push-pull - photographed from the footbridge at Stamford station on that late September day in 1965 - Ivatt 2-6-2T No.41219 of Leicester Midland shed. One of the original batch of twenty fitted with vacuum control gear by BR when new, the scruffy looking engine was condemned exactly one week after that last service had run. No.41212 survived just one week longer. Latterly three of the BR Standard version of the 2-6-2T, No.84005, 84006 and 84008, were used intermittently on the p&p from Seaton to Stamford but by the end of June 1965 they were all stored unserviceable at Leicester and never worked again. The bay on the left would have been the ideal place to run the p&p service to and from but by now a rake of goods vehicles blocked the line and the waiting time taken up by the train at Stamford did not obstruct any other trains passing through on the main line. Note the ornate woodwork of the awnings and the wonderful stone built accommodation of the main buildings on the opposite platform. Those same buildings survive to this day but in private use as a railway and transport bookshop. The goods shed appearing in the background was not so lucky as it was demolished at an unknown date after 1966 once the goods facility here was withdrawn. *BLP - DDLMS152.*

Southwell, March 1959: A Rolleston Junction train, with ex Johnson Midland 0-4-4T No.58065 as motive power - 'The Paddy', is about to leave Southwell on a dull day in March 1959. It may well seem dull for this service too. The transfers, in 1955, of the 0-4-4Ts (Nos.58077 and 58085 were involved at the time) from their small home at Southwell to the former Great Northern shed at Newark came to a head in early January 1959 when that shed closed too. Next the four-coupled tanks (No.58065 had replaced withdrawn No.58077 in September 1955) went off to Lincoln GN shed but their days on 'The Paddy' were numbered (No.58085 was condemned in March 1959). By mid-June 1959 the service was suspended; Southwell station, except for the occasional excursion, was closed. Note the new 21-ton capacity coal hopper wagons which, according to the painted notice on the side of Diagram 156 No.42945X, were dedicated to working between the newly commissioned Staythorpe power station (Staythorpe 'A' became fully operational in 1956, generating 336 megawatts, the 'B' station, of the same capacity, did not come fully on line until 1961) and whatever colliery they ended up at - 'Load only to Staythorpe Power Stn'. These hopper wagons were of course the precursors of the HAA high capacity 'Merry-go-round' wagons produced a few years later to service the vast base load power stations. So, here we see the ending of one service and the relative newness of another. However, even coal fired power stations don't last forever and the Staythorpe complex started to decommission by 1985 and the site is now being redeveloped as a new generation power station. *BLP - DHB992.* 27

This is Worksop with former London Tilbury & Southend 4-4-2T No.41943 heading a service to Mansfield. The picture is dated 12th October 1955! It seems highly unlikely to have had a fall of snow so early in the lead up to winter although this writer has experienced heavy snow on high ground in north-west England in late May and in northern Scotland during July. So, the date may in fact be correct; freaks of weather happen all the time in the United Kingdom. However, the engineman appears to have been prepared so perhaps the date is really 10/12/55! More to the point, the Mansfield based 3P tank engine is working its last winter before withdrawal. Apparently these engines were not very popular with their crews because the cabs got too hot! On this particular day such an extreme was probably most welcome. The last of four, later six, of its class allocated to Mansfield at Nationalisation, No.41943 and its ilk were replaced on the Worksop-Mansfield (Town)-Nottingham (Midland) services by Stanier 2-6-2Ts. Nowadays that same route, plied by those steam locomotives half a century ago, is now, after a thirty-year gap with no service, traversed by diesel multiple units and is marketed as the Robin Hood line. *BLP - DDLTS11.*

8Fs, 4Fs and a solitary 1F. No.41739 takes up just half of the stall inside Barrow Hill roundhouse at Staveley in March 1959. The half-cab 0-6-0T was one of a number of former MR tank engines designated to work the lines inside the Staveley works complex to which BR supplied with motive power via a long standing agreement made between the Midland Railway and the Staveley Iron Works. Along with classmates Nos.41706, 41708, 41710, 41734, 41752, 41763, 41769, 41803, 41804 and 41835, besides a handful of 0-4-0T engines of varying vintages, the 1F enjoyed permanent employment until withdrawal in June 1963. Five of the 1Fs carried on to the end of steam employment at the works in October 1965. *BLP - DHB990.*

Foxlow Junction - On Saturday 1st October 1966, the East Midlands branch of the RCTS staged a rail tour 'Notts. and Yorkshire Tour' over lines in both counties which rarely saw passenger trains. Colwick based Stanier Cl.5 No.44825, which had been suitably 'bulled-up' for the job, headed the train out of Nottingham (Midland) just after midday and then turned north onto the Leen valley lines to get up to the lines around Cresswell, Clowne and Seymour Junction. On the curve leading into Foxlow Junction the Cl.5 was replaced by a Brush Type 2 diesel, D5568, which then took the train onto the lines in and around the south Yorkshire colliery district. With RCTS members all over the place trying to get the best picture in the fading light, No.44825 is being uncoupled ready to make its way to Kirkby-in-Ashfield engine shed where it was serviced prior to rejoining the train at Shireoaks later that afternoon. Note that all six carriages of the train are in picture but most of the two hundred and thirty passengers are still aboard. With steam back in charge of the train the colliery areas east of Mansfield were traversed including the Clipstone west curve to Mansfield concentration sidings. After that, the train made its way back to Nottingham via the former Great Central main line into a ghostly Victoria station which had just two platforms in operation. At London Road High Level, a stop was made to set down a number of members but others stayed aboard for the final run to Netherfield & Colwick where No.44825 ran round and hauled the rail tour back to Nottingham centre and into Midland station. The heyday of the RCTS East Midlands branch organised rail tours was virtually over, the heady days of the early Sixties tours with special motive power gone, along with the steam locomotives once so numerous. *BLP - DD LMS448.*

Staveley Great Central. O4 No.63845 has charge of an Engineers Saloon in this May 1960 photograph taken from the Lowgates bridge at the south end of Staveley (Town [later Central]) station. Behind the coach, and diving out of sight, is the branch line to Ireland Colliery, to the right of which are the storage sidings for empty and full mineral wagons. To the right of those sidings and immediately south of them, but also out of sight, is Staveley's former LNER (Great Central) engine shed where the O4 resides. Of real interest in this picture is the long row of railway built cottages backing onto the Ireland branch. The cottages faced a similar long row on the same street which was, very appropriately, named Railway Cottages. The whole lot was built by the Manchester, Sheffield & Lincolnshire Railway when they chose Staveley to be the base from where they would strike out southwards during their making of the Great Central Railway and its London Extension. Of course, as we know, the GC is no more, the yards, sheds, and all the infrastructure associated with the railways here is long gone but the cottages are still home to dozens of families - albeit non-railway families for the most. However, the local council took over control of the properties some time ago and with no sign of a railway nearby, the council renamed the street Belmont Drive. The O4 Part 1 was one of the ex Ministry of Munitions engines purchased by the LNER in 1927. Its condition here is somewhat dubious but it plodded on for another year before it was called into Gorton and was then cut up. *BLP - DHB3518.*

The former Great Central engine shed at Staveley had quite a cosmopolitan atmosphere in March 1959 when Don Beecroft found this ex GE J69/2 tank, No.68591, on shed. The former GER 0-6-0Ts were no strangers to this place and had been allocated on numerous occasions; this one arrived from Stratford during the previous June. Besides the 0-6-0T there were the usual resident J11, O4, N5 and WD but joining them were a number of 350 h.p. 0-6-0 diesel shunters, stored 'Directors' and K2s from Darnall, along with visiting B16s from York and the inevitable B1. *BLP - DHB963.*

This is Kirkby yard in March 1965, as seen from the footbridge spanning the line towards Mansfield. Immediately below is 4F No.44401 at the head of a heavy coal train just out of the nearby Kirkby Colliery. The signal box controlling traffic to and from Kirkby Colliery sidings stood just behind the photographer. Tucked in between the 0-6-0 and its train is an unidentified 8F. This procession will be en route to Toton yard via Pye Bridge, Codnor Park and the Erewash line. The two engines are required to provide sufficient braking power for the heavy load of unfitted mineral wagons which will try its best to control the train down the gradients encountered along the line through Kirkby Woodhouse and Pinxton. Both steam and diesel locomotives are everyday sights at this location by late 1965, the latter becoming more common whilst the former are certainly diminishing. In view is another 8F, a 350 h.p. diesel shunter and a newly delivered Brush Type 4 Co-Co diesel-electric. Just prior to this scene being recorded, another 4F, No.44429 double-headed yet another 8F, No.48153, off to the south with another heavy coal train for Toton. Coal production in this area remained fairly constant for another twenty years or so, until the mid-eighties at least, but then wholesale closures saw the mines and the railways disappearing. After steam had gone from the area, Kirkby engine shed became a stabling point for diesel locomotives and at weekends especially, as many as thirty locomotives would rest in the yard. Double-heading continued too and pairs of English Electric Type 1 Bo-Bos became the norm in this part of the world. It was not unusual to see triple-heading with some trains. Note the B6021 road on the right; probably the busiest road in Kirkby-in-Ashfield during that period and look how quiet it appears. *BLP - DHB7341.*

This is Stanier 8F No.48541 at Kirkby-in-Ashfield engine shed in March 1966. This engine, and thirty-odd more of its classmates, formed the backbone of the heavy motive power pool at Kirkby. There usual task was to take coal trains from nearby collieries to the marshalling yard at Toton and return with empties. But even their brute strength was not enough to handle some of the heavy coal trains which had to be kept in check for the first section of the journey southwards (see Kirkby yard picture). By October 1966 steam power will have gone from 16G - ex 18B from September 1963 - and diesels will have taken over. Many of the surviving 8Fs, and 9Fs too, went chasing work over in Lancashire but No.48541 was condemned before then, in June, so never had the opportunity of steaming away from the place. *BLP - DHB7788.*

Having climbed up from the Erewash valley main line at Westhouses, 4F No.43865 blots out the sun as it continues the struggle whilst passing beneath the Great Central main line at Tibshelf in March 1965. The 0-6-0 was delivering empty mineral wagons from Toton Down yard to the former Stanton Iron Cos. coal mines at either Silverhill or Pleasley at Teversal, or Sutton Colliery which was situated on another branch about a mile south of Teversal. Note the mainly ash, rather than stone ballast, track bed employed on this route which was, by now, essentially a colliery branch, albeit well maintained. Up until the end of July 1930 a passenger station, known as Tibshelf & Newton, existed just beyond the bend which the rear of this train is negotiating. Opened by the Midland in 1886, it was initially called Tibshelf (Newton Road) but was some distance from the centre of Tibshelf. Three other stations, opened at the same time, also existed along the route which junctioned with the MR Mansfield-Worksop line at Mansfield Woodhouse: Whiteborough [the Ordnance Survey show this as City of Whiteborough], it was closed in October 1926; Teversal (Manor); and Pleasley (West), the latter two stations closed in July 1930 also. Our struggling 4F, a Westhouses engine, was condemned just a couple of months after this scene as captured. *BLP - DHB7343.*

In amongst the BR Standard 9Fs and the mounting piles of smokebox, firebox and ashpan debris, Annesley shed could field the occasional gem amongst it allocation of tender engines. On a cloudy Sunday in May 1960 this BR Derby-built Ivatt motor-fitted Class 2, No.41320, was having a sojourn from its normal duties working the depot's 'Dido' service. Arriving at 16D from Wellingborough in December 1959, the 2-6-2T was followed in January by No.41280 from Bedford. No.41227 arrived at Annesley in October 1961 to replace No.41320 which had transferred to the Southern Region but by April 1962 the remaining Ivatt's left the shed for Wellingborough, their job on the 'Dido' being taken over by their BR Standard Cl.2 counterparts, Nos.84006 and 84007 imported from Neasden and Wellingborough respectively. The BR 2-6-2Ts did not last too long on the workmen's train and after the summer workings were finished, a motor bus was used thereafter and, after a period doing carriage shunting at New Basford and e.c.s. workings into Nottingham (Victoria) station, the pair went into storage during September. A third BR Cl.2 (actually one of the initial pair, No.84006 replaced it) had transferred to Annesley in March 1962, No.84027, but on its arrival it was put into storage with a mechanical defect (there was never a requirement for more than two engines on the Dido duties anyway) and apparently never worked again being condemned in May 1964 after more than two years in store. So there we have, in a nutshell, the somewhat short and semi-tragic story of the Ivatt 2-6-2 tank engines' relationship with a particular Nottinghamshire motive power depot. *BLP - DHB3305.*

Quick! This ones' still got a nameplate on!. 'Royal Scot' No.46158 THE LOYAL REGIMENT rests on the shed yard at Annesley during the February 1963 period of the Big Freeze of 1962-63. Fully coaled and ready for its next duty on the Marylebone semi-fasts, the 4-6-0 still requires turning but that wouldn't take long. The reason why the engine was facing the wrong way for the next job was because the tender needed to be near to the shed in order to prevent the water freezing in the sub-zero air temperatures being experienced at that time. Note the trusty brazier working overtime alongside the water column. At this time there was eight 'Scots' allocated and working from Annesley but most had their nameplates removed so No.46158 was something of a rarity. By the following November it had become a complete rarity having been cut up at Crewe works after in October condemnation. *BLP - DHB6020.*

The north-easterly winds which brought the snow plastered to this melancholy bunch was extra cold and remained in place for weeks. This is February 1963 again but this lot are not getting any special treatment at Annesley shed. Instead, they are left to rot in the bitter conditions. You might wonder why so many of the same class, Thompson O1s, are huddled together and condemned in this exposed section of Nottinghamshire countryside. The truth is that none of the engines in view were unsound. Indeed, they should not have been withdrawn, never mind condemned. However, they were former Eastern Region and LNER stock and the London Midland Region had taken over their depot. Stanier 8Fs were quickly transferred into Annesley whilst the for GC 2-8-0s were laid up with indecent haste. Such was the politics of BR at the time, it was possible to scrap perfectly serviceable locomotives whilst introducing similar engines to do the same jobs. *BLP - DHB6019.*

A Nottingham (Midland) to Worksop via Mansfield (Town) stopping service is spotted traversing the old Midland metals at Hucknall in June 1960 with Stanier 2-6-2T No.40073 in charge. Now a resident of Kirkby-in-Ashfield shed, the Cl.3 mixed traffic tank had been evicted from its Mansfield depot on April Fools' Day 1960 after transferring from Llandudno Junction just six months previously. Like the earlier Fowler version of this design, the 2-6-2T did not live up to expectations and were therefore early casualties in British Railways endeavour to scrap everything fed by coal as soon as possible. By September 1962 No.40073 was condemned, its place on these services taken over by the much more successful 2-6-4T. However, two years later the passenger service itself was axed as part of The Beeching Plan and during the late evening of Saturday 10th October 1964 the last trains worked north and south along the route to end 115 years of passenger services. Mansfield was effectively cut off from the national passenger train network and for the next thirty years had the dubious distinction of being the largest town in England without a railway station. But common sense eventually prevailed and all is now different - see elsewhere in this album for the reason why. *BLP - DHB3534.*

Approximately halfway between Basford (Vernon) and Bulwell (Market) passenger stations, at the southern end of the former Midland Railway's Leen Valley line to Mansfield, the Great Northern Railway's Derby Extension line crossed over the MR formation via a spectacular lattice girder bridge (GNR bridge No.37) some 40ft above the rails. At one time, prior to WW2, there was attached to this south face, a pedestrian footbridge and evidence of its existence is shown by the three girder brackets still sticking out of the abutment just below the main girders. In October 1965, with the demise of the bridge not too far into the future, Stanier 8F No.48004 was captured performing one of its last duties and is heading north propelling a brakevan in order to collect another loaded coal train from one of the collieries situated in the aforementioned valley. The Kirkby-in-Ashfield based 2-8-0, one of the earliest built, in June 1935, was condemned at the end of the month. Situated just north of the sidings on the left there was another route diverging west, which once connected this MR secondary line to the Erewash valley main line. Much of that particular route had been closed and lifted some years ago to avoid the duplication so prevalent before and after Grouping. *BLP - DHB7728.*

Colwick based L1 No.67785 runs down the bank of the south to west curve from Bagthorpe Junction towards the train's next stop - Basford (North) - with an early afternoon service from Nottingham (Victoria) to Pinxton in June 1960. In the foreground is the shunting spur for Basford North goods yard whilst behind the last coach of the descending train can be seen carriages in the sidings situated between the curve and the former Great Central main line. Basford (North) enjoyed passenger services to Derby, Heanor and Pinxton besides the service to Nottingham (Victoria) but at the end of the summer timetable on 7th September 1964 the station closed to passenger traffic. The goods facility lasted a while longer to October 1967. The passenger service to Heanor had ceased as early as April 1928 but was used for some years afterwards by workmen's trains. Pinxton (or rather Pinxton South as British Railways re-christened the place in 1954) last virtually to the end but was obliterated from the railway network on 7th January 1963 when both passenger and goods services ceased. Today, much of the route from Awsworth junction, where the Pinxton branch left the Derby line, has been obliterated by nature, demolition and opencast mining. Basford North too has been erased from the map with housing taking the place of trains. *BLP - DHB3866.*

41

Heading for the Stanton Iron works at Ilkeston, in the Erewash valley, Austerity No.90037 wheels a heavy iron ore train over the junction at Basford North in October 1965. Having just worked up to Bagthorpe junction from the depths of Nottingham (Victoria) station, the WD then had the descent into Basford to contend with but the experienced crew of the 2-8-0 appear to be keeping the train in check as it joins the original Derbyshire Extension main line for its westward journey. Until the roof of Mapperley tunnel decided it wanted to join the trackbed running through it, trains such as this, which originated in the iron ore field south and east of the Vale of Belvoir, ran direct to Basford from Colwick along the so-called 'Back line'. However, when the tunnel was condemned in April 1960 all of the 'Back line' freight had to contend with a torturous routing through the 'Rat hole' at Bagthorpe junction, the descent through two tunnels into Victoria station, through Victoria Street tunnel, Weekday Cross junction, London Road High Level station and on to Sneinton and the main line to Colwick. By the date of this photograph the working of goods and passenger trains around this area of Nottingham was in rapid decline. New routes were being used or planned and this once busy railway junction was about to become history like the GN somersault signal in view. *BLP - DHB7733.*

A westbound mixed freight passes the rubbled remains of Kimberley station in April 1966 hauled by 8F 2-8-0 No.48690. The former Great Northern lines in this part of Nottinghamshire had been taken over by the London Midland Region some years before but the motive power, mainly supplied by Colwick shed, had kept an Eastern Region flavour until December 1965 when the LM authorities condemned or transferred away the remnants prior to their own Stanier products taking over. No.48690 was one of those Stanier engines and although 'ruling the roost' at Colwick, the external appearance reflects the contempt given to all BR steam at this time by the BR hierarchy. The rubble strewn about the place was once a passenger station but in September 1964, as the passenger services over the GN lines were curtailed, the stations closed and passed into history. This particular facility opened for business in August 1876 as part of the Great Northern's concerted push into Derbyshire to capture not just the passenger potential of the area but some of the lucrative coal traffic monopolised by the Midland Railway at that time. Besides the passenger station, the GN provided a goods depot here, complete with a 10-ton crane and livestock pens. The MR also had a station at Kimberley, on a near parallel route just north of the GN line, but the passenger station closed in 1917. *BLP - DHB7797.*

43

Another rail tour organised by the East Midlands branch of the RCTS on 19th September 1959, saw Ivatt Cl.2 tank No.41320 heading a couple of suburban coaches over various branches such as the long closed (to ordinary passenger services anyway) GNR Heanor branch from Ilkeston. In the distance can be seen the NCB screening plant where locally opencast mined coal was delivered to railway wagons until its closure in October 1963. The screens had been erected in 1940 by the Ministry of Fuel & Power to tap into the shallow coal reserves in the area. Considering the building of the plant was a war emergency measure, the twenty-three years continuous service it afterwards gave required a steam locomotive, with its own shed, to serve the adjacent sidings. The passenger station was closed by the LNER in May 1928 but four years later special workmen's trains ran until 1939 when they too succumbed. *BLP - DDLMS459.*

Over the years, the twin roundhouses at Derby stabled virtually everything the Midland built and pretty much many of the LMS Stanier designs. By the sixties it was stabling anything that would fit on its turntables including Type 3 main line diesel locomotives and the smaller shunting type. This 0-4-0 saddletank appears out of place suddenly although the rear of its cab has a likeness to early LMS diesel shunting locomotives - the Derby family resemblance perhaps. Although not a product of Derby works, being built by Kitsons in 1932, the little 0F tank was certainly a product of Derby drawing office where the first generation of LMS diesels were being designed. This view stems from about 1966 when the 0-4-0ST was in its last year of operation. Another species of LMS short wheelbase shunting engines, the ten members of this particular class managed to stay rooted in England but for much of their lives storage was the only thing on offer. It was surprising that No.47000 and three sister engines managed to get into 1966. *BLP - DDLMS632.*

On Sunday 28th October 1951 ex LMS Dock tank No.47166 had just completed at major overhaul at Derby works and is seen at the adjacent engine shed ready to start a short running-in routine which would prove that everything was working as it should be prior to returning home to Birkenhead. An unidentified but obviously ex-works 3F 0-6-0 stands behind the 2F 0-6-0T. Built at Derby in 1928 and 1929, the ten members of the class were scattered far and wide over the former LMS system, with three at Birkenhead, two in Edinburgh, two in Fleetwood, and three in Greenock. Although withdrawals started in 1959, it took six years before BR got rid of the last two in 1964. By that time the class had clocked up a few more sheds to their credit including Agecroft, Bidston, Bolton, Devons Road, Edge Hill, Hamilton, Speke Junction, Sutton Oak, Wrexham, and even Horwich works where Nos.47164 and 47165 had short careers but managed to become the last of the class, being withdrawn in September 1964. *BLP - DDLMS141.*

Although this picture of Stanier Class 5 No.44981 at Derby (Midland) station is undated, we can pin-point the date to a four year period between March 1955 and May 1959 when the 4-6-0 was allocated to 21B Bournville shed. The engine has worked in on what is either empty stock or an express consisting a varied mixture of carriages from numerous origins. *BLP - DDLMS206.*

47

Is this how we picture in our minds the typical pick-up goods? Leisurely shunting its wagons at a wayside station in bright sunshine? Well that's what was happening at Draycott & Breaston on a sunny afternoon in August 1959 as 4F No.44233 sorts its train with the shunter (guard) splitting and joining the various sections to drop off and pick-up the relevant wagons. Anybody who has observed events such as this will remember the long pauses between the engine moving backwards, then forwards, then backwards again with apparently very little changing; but things were changing with each movement. The slowness was sometimes mesmerising, perhaps even hypnotic. The fireman seems to have joined in with the mood and leans out of the cab with just enough stance to be comfortable and observant. It is all an age away now. Things (everything) move a little faster and not for the betterment of daily life. Whilst this task was being performed three expresses passed through here, the Up PALATINE with No.70017 ARROW in charge, a Lincoln-Derby train with No.61009 HARTEBEESTE at the helm, and a Down Manchester hauled by No.70021 MORNING STAR. Ironically the names of the locomotives were in some way connected with speed or swiftness but that was not going to affect this pick-up which required accuracy and deliberation to get it right. The station here, just visible on the left of the picture, was opened 1st April 1852. It closed to passengers, and goods 14th February 1966. The 4F was from Westhouses and must have been on one of that depot's plusher jobs. *BLP - DHB2712.*

As junctions go, Trent was certainly one of the biggest in the United Kingdom and its station somewhat unique in being able to serve trains from five different routes from one island platform. This is the North Junction in May 1960 although it may well have been 1920 or even sooner as it had not altered much since 1862 when the station here, known simply as Trent, was built. Royston based 3F 0-6-0 No.43681 heads a mixed freight onto the Nottingham route whilst crossing over the lines from Derby, which come in from the right. The track peeling off to the left of the locomotive was the Erewash valley main line to Toton yard, just over a mile or so to the north of this location. This goods train has just come from Derby but in order to find its way onto the Nottingham line it diverged right at Sawley junction to negotiate the sweeping curve taken by London bound passenger trains not calling at Trent. Although enjoying a reasonable passenger service, Trent station did not last as long as steam power on BR, closing on New Years Day 1968. Note the upper and lower quadrant signals protecting the same route but within fifty yards of each other. *BLP - DHB3523.*

49

The continuous flow of coal from the pits of the Derbyshire and Nottinghamshire coalfield witnessed in 1960 was a phenomena which had been taking place for over seventy-five years. At the time, it appeared that it would last for ever. Much of that coal was destined for markets south of those counties and so it was funnelled along the Erewash valley main line into Toton yard where it was sorted and despatched. On a daily basis, and sometimes more so, trainloads were sent to customers in London (north, south, east and west), Birmingham, Watford, Rugby, Bristol, Gloucester, Corby, Leicester, Banbury, to name but a few. The list was comprehensive but the marshalling at Toton went on around the clock so that dozens and dozens of trains could deliver the 'black gold'. To feed the appetite of the yard, engine sheds along the Erewash valley kept fleets of 2F, 3F, and 4F 0-6-0s, 8F 2-8-0s and once, a number of the mighty Garratts too, busy emptying colliery yards and returning with empties from Toton Down yard. Westhouse based 3F 0-6-0 No.43825 was one of the hundreds of locomotives employed in the coal business and here at Langley Mill, in July 1960, it is seen heading another train of mineral wagons bound for Toton's Up yard. The train is running on the Up Slow, with the Down Slow alongside. The fast lines are nearer the camera. *BLP - DHB4021.*

50

Now here is a fairly rare occurrence on the Midland main line through the Erewash valley - a Thompson B1 in charge of a St Pancras to Bradford relief. The location is Ilkeston Junction, just north of the point where the Erewash river leaves the company of the Erewash canal and dives beneath the main line to run parallel with the Nottingham canal before flowing beneath the main line again near Trowell station. The date is sometime during August 1961. It is highly probable that the B1 was put on the train at Nottingham or perhaps even Leicester. It is highly improbable to have worked the train from London. However, at this time the 4-6-0 was a new acquisition of Millhouses shed and it may well have got to London on one of the numerous expresses originating from Sheffield (Midland). There is no reason why 41C did not utilise the engine because it was quite capable and if one of their 'Jubilees' had gone sick at the last minute. All theory of course but someone would know the facts. Nevertheless, the young 'spotters' holding onto the gate must have been taken aback by the appearance of this foreigner rushing past their perch. As for the stock, that alone must have been worth a second glance, never mind the motive power. *BLP - DHB5539.*

Seen from the same footbridge but some twelve months beforehand, the more usual fare of a 'Royal Scot' shatters the early evening silence with a Down Edinburgh relief in August 1960. A rather clean No.46123 ROYAL IRISH FUSILIER, from Kentish Town shed, seems to be making light work of the ten-coach load. The 4-6-0 would have worked this train as far as Leeds where a change of engine would take place, the 'Scot' working back home the next day after a night on Holbeck shed. This would have been the last summer when this locomotive would look anything like decent. Twelve months hence and Saltley had the services of No.46123 but none of their jobs entailed work like this so the 'namer' was relegated to secondary duties and storage. At the end of June 1962 a recall to top class main line work at Upperby shed had the 'Scot' working over the West Coast Main Line again, the place where it had spent most of its life. But age caught up with the high mileage engine and during the following November it was condemned. One last trip along the WCML, albeit in tow, took it to Crewe works and oblivion in May 1963. *BLP - DHB4240.*

52

Passing a northbound coal empties at Ilkeston Junction, 'Jubilee' No.45561 SASKATCHEWAN (the name that everybody could pronounce but could not spell) has charge of a southbound relief from Bradford to St Pancras in August 1960. Travelling along the Up Fast, the Kentish Town 6P will soon start to slow for the junction at Trowell where it would diverge towards Nottingham. No.45561 appears ex-works but the shine has been applied at its own shed. In the background, looking like something you would certainly find in Australia, but less permanent, was the spoil heap from a colliery at Cossall. Nowadays such a sighting on the horizon might raise a few eyebrows but in 1960 they were everywhere throughout the coalfields - monuments to a century of hard labour. Without doubt, the Erewash valley line was an interesting route for the traveller, coal mining, heavy industry, railway lines and associated infrastructure everywhere, canals, a river meandering from one side of the valley to the next. Today it is but a shadow of what it used to be but at least we have photographic images such as these to help us understand how it looked and worked. *BLP - DHB4237.*

The footbridge from where a number of the images at Ilkeston were captured, is featured in this August 1961 view of 4F 0-6-0 No.44106 heading towards Toton with - coal - what else. The engine is showing reporting number, or target, No.84 on the right of the bufferbeam, presumably one of Toton's myriad of duties. The photographer is standing on the wooden crossing where it bisects the Up Fast! *BLP - DHB5531.*

This could be the Lickey incline - if you allow your eye follow the carriages back to the rear of the train - well, maybe but this view does have a flavour of that famous bank. 'Jubilee' No.45602 BRITISH HONDURAS has charge of a Bradford-St Pancras express in early October 1958 and has just topped the bank at Trowell summit after wheeling its train off the Erewash valley main line to make its way to its next stop - Nottingham (Midland). The Millhouses engine appears to be steaming well with plenty to spare although its romp from Chesterfield would hardly have taxed the capacity of the 6Ps boiler. *BLP - DHB2872.*

Look carefully at this Down goods passing Stanton Gate behind Cl.4 No.43125 in May 1966. Long isn't it. Admitted it is made up mainly of empty mineral wagons but nevertheless it is a substantial train for the mixed traffic 2-6-0. Some distance away from its usual habitat around the West Riding, the Normanton engine appears to be in fine fettle and is steaming nicely too. This particular Ivatt mogul spent all of its short sixteen year life allocated to sheds in the North Eastern Region of BR, and it was at Normanton in September 1967 that it was withdrawn albeit because steam was banished from that time on the Eastern/North Eastern Region. It would be nice to know how far No.43125 worked this train - perhaps all the way home which I would like to think it did. Now note the sidings on the Down side of the main line and the signal box controlling trains which crossed from the siding on the Up side (obscured by the mogul and its train). These sidings dealt with trains arriving and departing from the Stanton Iron Co. works which were situated behind and to the right of the photographer. Because most express passenger trains traversing the Erewash valley line joined or left the main line north of here at Trowell, to serve Nottingham, the chances of conflicting movements spoiling a passenger train schedule at this spot were minimal. *BLP - DHB7833.*

It wasn't all 4F 0-6-0s and 8F 2-8-0s hauling coal from the Notts./Derby coalfield into Toton yard - at least not by 1966 when diesels had taken over much of the coal traffic. This is BR Standard Cl.4 No.75011 passing through Stapleford & Sandiacre station in May 1966 with a coal train from the north. The Skipton based 4-6-0 is nearing its destination with this load but is someway off its normal sphere of operations, so must have been 'borrowed' by either Westhouses, Canklow or even Hasland to bring this loaded train to Toton yard. Steam locomotive servicing at Toton shed could only be described as minimal by this time so once released from the reception sidings, the Cl.4 would have to make do with a drink from a column and then head north with empties or light engine. When its withdrawal took place in November 1966, No.75011 was just fifteen years old. This photographically recorded event at Stapleford & Sandiacre took place nearly forty-five years ago. Since then the passenger station has closed (2nd January 1967, just five years short of its centenary), the vast marshalling yard at Toton is now simply a dumping and storage point for wagons and redundant diesel locomotives. The adjacent diesel depot is still doing good business and nowadays undertakes major overhauls of its charges, something not quite envisaged when constructed in the mid-sixties. Of course, the coal traffic has dried up, the British coal mining industry being all but wiped off the map but a succession of political and geological upheavals. Oh! And that's the old A52 trunk road running over the bridge. *BLP - DHB7852.*

Six years earlier, in July 1960, the goods yard at Stapleford & Sandiacre hosted ex Midland 2F 0-6-0 No.58214 which is seen resting after a spot of shunting. The ancient 2F was part of the Toton allocation but was a newcomer to that depot having arrived from Bedford during the previous month. A year later it went to Coalville but it was by then in a run down condition, and due to a boiler change at least. Entering Derby works in February 1962, it was observed lying on Foundry Row on Monday 19th of that month, awaiting cut-up, along with three 3F 0-6-0Ts. No.58214 left Derby in little pieces, its usefulness having ceased some months before. *BLP - DHB4030.*

Pictures of this engine do not turn up very often, especially at its home shed - 16A Nottingham. The date is 25th May 1962 and 'Scot' No.46100 ROYAL SCOT is looking rather clean whilst standing on the ash wagon road - I can't believe it is on shed pilot duties but who knows? Maybe it was! More than likely it was parked 'out-of-the-way' to await its next duty which would appear to be a northbound working. With just over four months to go before withdrawal, and eventual preservation, the 7P is looking resplendent and is a credit to the Nottingham shed staff to whom it had been in care since November 1959. *BLP - DDLMS214.*

Locally based B1 No.61092 waits at the signal, at the south end of platform No.7, for the route to Colwick depot whilst on the centre road, or middle siding as it was officially known, between platforms 7 and 4, 'Hall' No.6911 HOLKER HALL gets the right-of-way which will enable it to reverse into the Victoria Street tunnel prior to setting back to use the turntable in the servicing yard, which was situated in the south-east corner of the station, alongside the south dock. The Banbury based 4-6-0 has brought in the Saturdays Only Poole-Bradford express (1N63), a regular working for these most welcome visitors and one which brought them to Nottingham from July 1964 onwards as the former engine changing point from Western to Midland Region locomotives was moved northwards to Nottingham after the ex Great Central shed closed at Leicester. Besides the aforementioned express the Bournemouth-York was another which brought a 'Hall' or occasionally a 'Grange' to Victoria. Of course the oft told story of one such engine - No.6858 - getting as far as Huddersfield, has been well documented but, to many enthusiasts, the fact that former Great Western locomotives worked into Nottingham nearly every day for the two years from the summer of 1964 until virtually the end of the GC route, is something worth savouring. Towards the end of the workings, in 1966 and also in 1965, diesels deputised for steam; Class 37 and 47 being the usual fare. *BLP - DDGWR319.*

"This is the only problem with this working!" As the driver might be saying to his fireman as they push the manually operated turntable round 180 degrees at the Victoria locomotive servicing area in August 1964. There was not a lot of room left on the rails of the turntable, especially when the 100-ton plus load had to be balanced just right with just a few inches to play with. Of course a couple of locomotives came unstuck on this table and overshot, breaking through the bufferstop and dumping their tenders onto the ground. However, No.6911 appears to be behaving today. Nevertheless it was hard work. *BLP - DDGWR323.*

A panoramic view at the south end of a very quiet Nottingham (Victoria) at some time in the mid-sixties [The engine was allocated to 1G from 8/63 to 1/65]. BR Standard Cl.5 No.73071 (Woodford Halse) stands at the head of a rake of suburban stock in the middle siding between the Up and Down Fast platforms, Nos.7 and 4 respectively. At the north end of the same siding another tender

62

engine stands as station pilot. Eventually the Standard will take the stock out of the middle road, run into the Victoria Street tunnel and then reverse the whole lot into platform 7 to form a stopping service to Rugby. In the meantime, like the schoolboys on the platform trolley, the Standard 5 awaits something faster coming in from the north. *BLP - DDBRS45.*

A summers evening view of the south end of Victoria station looking north-west with the clock tower and hotel building casting shadows over the train shed. A Derby Lightweight d.m.u., on a Grantham service, departs platform No.12 whilst a handful of spotters hang around for a possible 'cop' which might work through the station. *BLP - DDBRD426.*

A rare visitor to Nottingham (Victoria) was Britannia Pacific No.70004 WILLIAM SHAKESPEARE. In this undated (thought to be 1964) photograph at the south end of the station, the 'locals' are certainly giving it some attention as it works what appears to be a diverted service. During the period in question, No.70004 was allocated to Willesden so would not be involved (except in case of failure) with any of the Marylebone services. Nevertheless, whatever the circumstances, the photograph is certainly a memorable sight. *BLP - DDBRS292.*

65

The apparent 'last day' at Nottingham (Victoria) brought out a fair crowd, mainly railway enthusiasts and local historians. This view of the south end bay platforms Nos.5 and 6 (with the 3-car Cravens built Diesel Multiple Unit departing No.6) shows interested parties observing, photographing and travelling on the train which I think was a stopping service bound for Rugby. Note the foliage growing up through the sleepers, especially along the edge of platform 6 - obviously the weed killing train left this place off its rounds a couple of years previously. It was a day of mixed feelings for Nottingham. There were those who relished the modernisation of the city centre and the coming of a shopping centre which promised a new shopping experience, inside a mall with piped music, bright lighting and all the big name shops. Others, would miss the Victorian architecture and ambience of the station. The train service was never much to write home about and Midland station could handle some of the traffic, the rest would be lost but that is the price of moving on, advancement, progress. Were you there? *BLP - DDBRD427.*

The 'new order' never really had a chance to consolidate its foothold at Nottingham (Victoria) but nevertheless the diesels arrived and departed in between steam as though nothing was amiss. This is Brush Type 4 Co-Co D1572 at the head of a northbound express in 1966. During July of the following summer the station was relegated from the League proper when it became an unstaffed halt; final closure taking place on 4th September. Are those condemned coaches in the bay platform on the Up side? *BLP - DDBRD12.*

This is Weekday Cross, Nottingham. The date is sometime in 1966. A stopping train from Leicester approaches the junction behind an unidentified Stanier Cl.5, a class which by now dominates the remaining passenger services on this former Great Central route to Leicester, Rugby and London. Closure of the line hereabouts is pencilled in for September 1967 and Victoria station, beyond the tunnel behind the camera, will be demolished soon afterwards. However, the line branching off to the left, to Nottingham (London Road High Level) and on to Colwick and Grantham, will remain open for some time afterwards to allow dedicated freight traffic to run to and from a gypsum plant at Ruddington on the GC route. For this particular working, which required reversing the trains, the Victoria Street tunnel was bricked up at its north end (work on the Victoria Shopping Centre then started uninterrupted by any railway lines), buffer stops were erected at the north end of the tunnel and the tracks therein were treated as sidings. In May 1968 the signal box was closed then demolished. The tracks were singled in 1973 to allow the laying of heating pipes from a nearby incinerator plant to supply the city centre with warmth. In April 1974 the real end came for this section of the GCR route as the gypsum traffic was sent via a new connection south of the plant. The remaining trackwork here was taken up and demolition of the high level viaducts followed. Of course renewal in the form of the Nottingham tram system has seen a new tram terminus built on the alignment of the GC route, the tram tracks coming in from a point just to the right front of the camera position here. Long may the tram live and hopefully expand southwards across the Trent and into the southern suburbs of Nottingham. *BLP - DDLMS595.*

On a warm June evening in 1966, Stanier Class 5 No.45464 saunters past Wilford brickyard with the 6.15 p.m. departure from Nottingham (Victoria) to Rugby (Central). With just over a year to go before Victoria closes on 4th September 1967, the place is already taking on an ambience of doom. To service the GC line passenger traffic south of Nottingham after that date, Arkwright Street was reopened and remained so until 5th May 1969 when the whole line and its stations, including Rugby, were axed and the GC was no more. Of course sections remained intact for some years after closure and enthusiasts groups took advantage of the surviving infrastructure to bring parts of the old main line back to life. *BLP - DHB7861.*

69

The effects of the long cold winter were still being felt in March 1963 but on clear days the sun did its best to lift the gloom prior to the opening of spring. At the semi-derelict Edwalton station on the London Midland Region's Nottingham to Melton Mowbray line, 'Jubilee' No.45695 MINOTAUR runs through effortlessly and, it appears, with steam to spare, with a Down fitted freight in the early afternoon. Opened in February 1880, this former Midland station closed at the end of July 1941. Miraculously the building, and much of the roof, was still intact twenty-odd years on. After this particular route was closed by British Railways, a section of the line near Old Dalby was used as a test track. *BLP - DHB6044.*

Walking south along the platform for a little way and then turning about, the photographer now has a good view of the line coming in from Nottingham. Obviously from the way Stanier 8F No.48335 is performing with its heavy coal train, the gradient is against it and a good exhaust is blown over towards the sparsely populated area immediately to the east of the line. If a footbridge existed at this place it was long gone by 1963, its continual upkeep would have been a drain on scarce financial resources. Of course, if it been a metal bridge, the chances are it was purloined by the Government as scrap during the war period. It is quite possible - but something of a long shot - that the metal from the bridge was used in the making of this 2-8-0, which was one of the Horwich built members of the class from 1943! *BLP - DHB6045.*

Just to the south of the erstwhile Edwalton station, the A606 trunk road crosses the railway on a skew bridge. The bridge offered a decent vantage point to photograph the passing trains. Such advantage was taken in March 1963 when this 'Peak', D20, was accelerating away from Nottingham with an afternoon service (1M24) to St Pancras via Melton, Oakham and Corby (the slow way to London). Note the goods shed in the distance and the buffers of the headshunt adjacent to the position of the diesel. It is not known when the goods facility closed at this place but looking at the ground signal and the points beneath the Type 4, it may well have bee operational still in 1963. Nearby was a brickworks (Smarts) which used the goods yard and its railway service for a number of years. Photographic evidence from August 1962 shows 16-ton mineral wagons in the sidings and coal merchants using the yard for their trade. On the left, the siding there was being used for the age old business of stabling semi-redundant (only brought out for excursions or emergency) coaches. One final point, these particular Type 4 diesel-electrics were amongst the quietest on British Railways and their approach was not always noted audibly, especially when they were going fast such as this. In aviation circles, shortly before the advent of commercial jet airliners the Bristol Britannia was popularly known as 'The Whispering Giant'. The same label could have been attached to these 138-ton monsters. *BLP - DHB6043.*